# ABC and abc

## NAME: _____

A B C D E F G H I J K L M
N O P Q R S T U V W X Y Z
a b c d e f g h i j k l m n
o p q r s t u v w x y z

Write ALL the ABCs and abcs!

**A** _____

_____

**a** _____

_____

# CAT

cat cat cat cat cat cat
cat cat cat
cat cat cat
cat cat cat

Write "cat" on the lines:

**cat**_____

_____

Circle the "cats"

cap    (cat)    cap    cat

cat    cat    cut    can

# I SEE A CAT

NAME: _____

I see a cat.
I see a cat.
I see a cat.

I see a cat.  <u>I see a cat</u>

I see a cat.  _____

I see a cat.  _____

I see a cat.  _____

I see a cat.  _____

I see a cat.  _____

I see a cat.  _____

# BED

NAME: _____

bed bed bed
bed bed bed
bed bed bed

Write "bed" on the lines:

## bed _____

_____

Circle the "beds"

bed     bed     cat     red

bed     bad     bag     bed

# THE BED IS RED

NAME: _____

The bed is red.
The bed is red.
The bed is red.
The bed is red.
The bed is red.
The bed is red.
The bed is red.
The bed is red.
The bed is red.
The bed is red.

_____

_____

_____

_____

_____

_____

# PIG

pig pig pig pig pig pig
pig                        pig
pig                     pig
pig pig                pig pig

Write "pig" on the lines:

**pig** _____

_____

Circle the "pigs"

rip      big      pig      pit

pig      pig      pin      hip

# THE PIG IS BIG

NAME: _____

The pig is big.
The pig is big.
The pig is big.
The pig is big.
The pig is big.
The pig is big.
The pig is big.
The pig is big.
The pig is big.

_____

_____

_____

_____

_____

_____

# DOG

NAME: _____

dog dog dog
dog dog dog
dog dog dog
dog dog dog dog dog

Write "dog" on the lines:

## dog _____

_____

Circle the "dogs"

ham     cat     jog     men

rat     dog     pen     dog

# I SEE A DOG

NAME: _____

I see a dog.
I see a dog.
I see a dog.
I see a dog.
I see a dog.
I see a dog.
I see a dog.
I see a dog.
I see a dog.
I see a dog.
I see a dog.

# BUG

NAME: _____

bug bug bug bug bug
bug bug bug bug bug
bug bug bug
bug bug bug

Write "bug" on the lines:

**bug** _____

_____

Circle the "bugs"

| big | pen | bug | bag |
|-----|-----|-----|-----|
| bag | bug | pen | bug |

# I SEE A BUG

NAME: _____

I see a bug.
I see a bug.
I see a bug.
I see a bug.
I see a bug.
I see a bug.
I see a bug.
I see a bug.
I see a bug.

_____

_____

_____

_____

_____

_____

# BAG

NAME: _____

bag bag bag
bag bag bag
bag bag bag
bag bag bag bag bag

Write "bag" on the lines:

<u>bag</u>_____

_____

Circle the "bags"

big    bag    gum    bus

bag    bug    gas    bag

# HE HAS A BAG

NAME: _____

He has a bag.
He has a bag.
He has a bag.
He has a bag.
He has a bag.
He has a bag.
He has a bag.
He has a bag.
He has a bag.
He has a bag.

_____

_____

_____

_____

_____

_____

_____

# HEN

NAME: _____

hen hen hen
hen hen hen
hen hen hen
hen hen hen

Write "hen" on the lines:

## hen _____

_____

Circle the "hens"

pen    men    hen    hug

hen    hen    pen    ten

# THE HEN IS BIG

NAME: _____

The hen is big.
The hen is big.
The hen is big.

_____

_____

_____

_____

_____

_____

_____

# LIP

lip lip lip lip lip lip lip lip
lip lip                    lip lip
lip lip                    lip lip
lip lip lip          lip lip lip

Write "lip" on the lines:

## lip
_____

_____

Circle the "lips"

rip     rip     lip     rip

lip     lip     pin     hip

# I HAVE TWO LIPS

NAME: _____

I have two lips.
I have two lips.
I have two lips.

# MOP

NAME: _____

mop        mop mop

mop  mop        mop mop

mop  mop        mop mop

mop  mop  mop  mop  mop

Write "mop" on the lines:

## mop _____

_____

Circle the "mops"

pop    men    mop    hug

mop    mop    top    hop

# THE MOP IS WET

NAME: _____

The mop is wet.
The mop is wet.
The mop is wet.

_____

_____

_____

_____

_____

_____

_____

# BUS

bus bus       bus

bus bus       bus

bus bus    bus bus

bus bus bus bus bus

Write "bus" on the lines:

**bus**_____

_____

Circle the "buses"

bag     bus     bug     big

bus     big     bus     bus

# THE BUS IS BIG

NAME: _____

The bus is big.
The bus is big.
The bus is big.

_____

_____

_____

_____

_____

_____

_____

# HAM

ham ham ham ham ham
ham ham ham
ham ham ham
ham ham ham

Write "ham" on the lines:

**ham** _____

_____

Circle the "hams"

him  bag  jam  ham

ham  ham  nap  hop

# THE HAM IS GOOD

NAME: _____

The ham is good.
The ham is good.
The ham is good.

_____

_____

_____

_____

_____

_____

_____

# PEN

pen pen pen pen pen
pen pen pen
pen pen pen
pen pen pen

Write "pen" on the lines:

**pen**_____

_____

Circle the "pens"

| pan | pig | hen | pen |
|-----|-----|-----|-----|
| pen | pen | pan | men |

# I HAVE A PEN

NAME: _____

I have a pen.
I have a pen.
I have a pen.

_____

_____

_____

_____

_____

_____

_____

_____

# SIT

NAME: _____

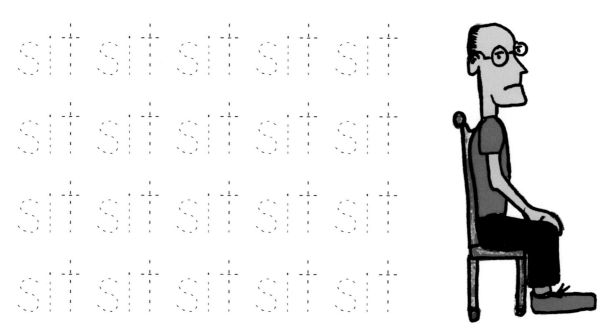

Write "sit" on the lines:

**sit**_____

_____

Circle the "sits"

hit    sit    sit    sit

net    pin    win    hit

# I SIT DOWN

NAME: _____

I sit down.
I sit down.
I sit down.

_____

_____

_____

_____

_____

_____

_____

# POP

NAME: _____

pop pop pop pop
pop pop pop pop
pop pop pop pop
pop pop pop pop

Write "pop" on the lines:

**pop**_____

_____

Circle the "pops"

pop    pen    pop    mop    hop

pool    pop    pop    pen    top

# I LIKE POP

NAME: _____

I like pop.
I like pop.
I like pop.

_____

_____

_____

_____

_____

_____

_____

_____

# SUN

NAME: _____

sun sun sun sun sun
sun                    sun sun
sun                    sun sun
sun                    sun sun

Write "sun" on the lines:

## sun_____

_____

Circle the "suns"

sun     see     sun     run     star

fun     sun     run     pen     bun

# I SEE THE SUN

NAME: _____

I see the sun.
I see the sun.
I see the sun.

_____

_____

_____

_____

_____

_____

_____

_____

# BAT

NAME: _____

bat bat bat   bat bat
bat            bat bat
bat            bat bat
bat bat bat bat bat bat

Write "bat" on the lines:

**bat**_____

_____

Circle the "bats"

bat   pen   bat   big   bat

sat   bat   hat   mat   cat

# A BAT IS SMALL

NAME: _____

A bat is small.
A bat is small.
A bat is small.

_____

_____

_____

_____

_____

_____

_____

_____

# JET

NAME: _____

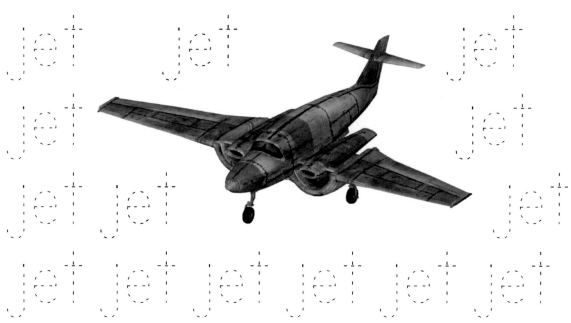

Write "jet" on the lines:

**jet** _____

_____

Circle the "jets"

jazz   get   jet   jet   jam

get   jet   jet   jam   jet

# A JET IS FAST

NAME: _____

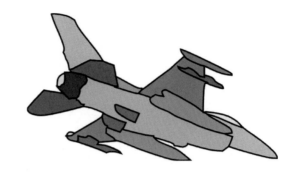

A Jet is fast.
A Jet is fast.
A Jet is fast.

_____

_____

_____

_____

_____

_____

_____

# HAT

NAME: _____

hat hat    hat  hat
hat                 hat hat
hat                 hat hat
hat hat hat hat hat hat

Write "hat" on the lines:

## hat_____

_____

Circle the "hats"

cat    sat    hat    hat    hot

mat    hat    rat    fat    hat

# IT IS MY HAT

NAME: _____

It is my hat.
It is my hat.
It is my hat.

_____

_____

_____

_____

_____

_____

_____

# CUP

cup cup cup cup cup
cup cup cup cup
cup cup cup cup
cup cup cup cup cup

Write "cup" on the lines:

## cup _____

_____

Circle the "cups"

hug     bus     cup     hug     cup

bug     cup     bug     cup     mug

# I HAVE A CUP

NAME: _____

I have a cup.
I have a cup.
I have a cup.

_____

_____

_____

_____

_____

_____

_____

# POT

NAME: _____

*pot pot pot pot pot*
*pot pot*
*pot pot*
*pot pot pot*

Write "pot" on the lines:

## pot

Circle the "pots"

| | | | |
|---|---|---|---|
| pot | hot | pet | pet |
| pen | pot | not | pot |

# I NEED A POT

NAME: _____

I need a pot.
I need a pot.
I need a pot.

_____

_____

_____

_____

_____

_____

_____

# RUN

NAME: _____

run run run
run run run
run run run run run
run run run run run

Write "run" on the lines:

**run**_____

_____

Circle the "runs"

tub   run   bun   rub

run   fun   sun   run

# I CAN RUN

NAME: _____

I can run.
I can run.
I can run.

_____

_____

_____

_____

_____

_____

_____

# TEN

NAME: _____

10

ten ten ten
ten ten ten
ten ten ten ten ten ten
ten ten ten ten ten ten

Write "ten" on the lines:

## ten_____

_____

Circle the "tens"

net    hen    hit    pen

ten    tent    net    ten

# I HAVE TEN

NAME: _____

I have ten toes.
I have ten toes.
I have ten toes.

_____

_____

_____

I have ten. _____
You have ten. _____
He has ten. _____
She has ten. _____

# SIX

NAME: _____

six six six six
six six six six
six six six six
six six six six six six

Write "six" on the lines:

## six _____

_____

Circle the "sixes"

six     six     sit     six

fix     sit     six     fox

# I AM SIX

NAME: _____

I am six years old.
I am six years old.
I am six years old.

_____

_____

_____

I am six. _____
You are six. _____
He is six. _____
She is six. _____

# JAM

NAME: _____

Jam Jam Jam Jam
Jam Jam Jam Jam
Jam Jam Jam Jam
Jam Jam Jam Jam Jam

Write "jam" on the lines:

jam _____

_____

Circle the "jams"

jet    jam    get    jam

jar    can    jam    man

# I EAT JAM

## NAME: _____

I eat jam.
I eat jam.
I eat jam.

_____

_____

_____

Jam is red. _____
Jam is sweet. _____
I like jam. _____
Do you like jam? _____

# CAN

can can can can can
can can     can can
can can     can can
can can     can can

Write "can" on the lines:

**can**_____

_____

Circle the "cans"

cap    can     car     can

cat    can     can     man

# I HAVE A CAN

NAME: _____

I have a can.
I have a can.
I have a can.

_____

_____

_____

I have a can of cola.

_____

I have a can of juice.

_____

# SAD

NAME: _____

Write "sad" on the lines:

**sad**_____

_____

Circle the "sads"

cat    sad     sad     sad

sat    can     sad     bad

# I FEEL SAD

NAME: _____

I feel sad.
I feel sad.
I feel sad.

_____

_____

_____

I have no cake.

_____

I have no donuts.

_____

# MAP

NAME: _____

map map map

map map map

map map map map map

map map map map map

Write "map" on the lines:

**map**_____

_____

Circle the "maps"

nap     pan     man     map

tap     cap     map     man

# I HAVE A MAP

## NAME: _____

I have a map.
I have a map.
I have a map.

_____

_____

_____

I find my city.

_____

I find my house.

_____

# PIN

NAME: _____

pin pin pin pin pin
pin pin pin pin pin
pin pin pin pin pin
pin pin pin pin pin

Write "pin" on the lines:

pin_____

_____

Circle the "pins"

pink    pin    pin    pin

pan    pen    pin    pan

# I HAVE PINS

NAME: _____

I have pins.
I have pins.
I have pins.

_____

_____

_____

I have blue pins.

_____

I have yellow pins.

_____

# RUB

NAME: _____

rub rub rub
rub rub rub
rub rub rub
rub rub rub rub rub

Write "rub" on the lines:

**rub**_____

_____

Circle the "rubs"

tub    rub    bun    rub

run    fun    rub    rub

# I RUB MY SHOE

NAME: _____

I rub my shoe.
I rub my shoe.
I rub my shoe.

_____

_____

_____

My shoe is black.

_____

My shoe is brown.

_____

# PAN

NAME: _____

pan pan pan pan
pan pan pan
pan pan pan pan
pan pan pan pan pan

Write "pan" on the lines:

**pan**_____

_____

Circle the "pans"

pen  pan  pan  pan  pin

can  pen  pan  pat  pot

# I USE A PAN

NAME: _____

I use a pan.
I use a pan.
I use a pan.

_____

_____

_____

I fry eggs.

_____

I fry bacon.

_____

# SUB

NAME: _____

sub     sub sub sub

sub     sub sub

sub     sub sub

sub sub sub sub sub

Write "sub" on the lines:

**sub**_____

_____

Circle the "subs"

tub     sub     bun     rub

run     fun     sun     sub

# I SEE A SUB

NAME: _____

I see a sub.
I see a sub.
I see a sub.

_____

_____

_____

The sub is cool.

_____

The sub is in the sea.

_____

# WIN

win win win win win win
win win win win
win win win win
win win win win

Write "win" on the lines:

## win_____

_____

Circle the "wins"

pin    wind    hit    win

wind    pig    win    win

# I CAN WIN

NAME: _____

I can win.
I can win.
I can win.

_____

_____

_____

I can run and I can win.

_____

I can jump and I can win.

_____

# BUN

bun bun bun
bun bun bun
bun bun bun
bun bun bun bun bun

Write "bun" on the lines:

## bun_____

_____

Circle the "buns"

tub   bun   bun   bus

bun   fun   sun   bun

# I HAVE A BUN

NAME: _____

I have a bun.
I have a bun.
I have a bun.

_____

_____

_____

I have a bun for hotdogs.

_____

I have a bun for hamburgers.

_____

# NAME: _____

wind wind wind wind
wind            wind
wind            wind
wind      wind wind

Write "wind" on the lines:

## wind_____

_____

Circle the "winds"

jump     wind     cars     wind

wind     win     slip     win

# IT IS SO WINDY

NAME: _____

It is so windy.
It is so windy.
It is so windy.

_____

_____

_____

It is so rainy too.

_____

It is so cold too.

_____

# GET

NAME: _____

Write "get" on the lines:

<u>get_____</u>

_____

Circle the "gets"

## jet    get    gum    go
## get    met    gas    get

# I GET A TOY!

NAME: _____

I get a toy !
I get a toy !
I get a toy !

_____

_____

_____

I get a new doll. _____
I get a new truck. _____
I get a new game. _____
I get a new book. _____

# WEB

NAME: _____

web web web

web web web

web web web web web

web web web web web

Write "web" on the lines:

## web_____

_____

Circle the "webs"

set    web    net    web

get    net    web    wet

# I SEE A WEB

NAME: _____

I see a web.
I see a web.
I see a web.

_____

_____

_____

I see a spider. _____
I see a fly. _____
Spiders eat flies. _____
I like bugs. _____

# VET

vet vet vet vet vet vet
vet vet vet vet
vet vet vet vet
vet vet vet vet

Write "vet" on the lines:

## vet_____

_____

Circle the "vets"

| set | vet | net | vet |
|-----|-----|-----|-----|
| get | net | vet | wet |

# MY VET IS NICE

NAME: _____

My vet is nice.
My vet is nice.
My vet is nice.

_____

_____

_____

My vet likes cats. _____
My vet likes dogs. _____
My vet likes fish. _____
My vet likes birds. _____

# HAND

hand hand
hand hand
hand hand hand hand
hand hand hand hand

Write "hand" on the lines:

## hand

_____

Circle the "hands"

hand    hang    band    hand

band    stand    hand    hand

# I HAVE TWO HANDS

## NAME: _____

I have two hands.
I have two hands.
I have two hands.

_____

_____

_____

I hold a cat. _____
I hold a bird. _____
I hold a ball. _____
I hold a pen. _____

# LAMP

NAME: _____

lamp lamp lamp
lamp lamp lamp
lamp lamp lamp
lamp lamp lamp lamp

Write "lamp" on the lines:

## lamp _____

_____

Circle the "lamps"

lamb    camp    ramp    lamp

lamb    stamp    lamp    lamp

# I HAVE A RED LAMP

### NAME: _____

I have a red lamp.

I have a red lamp.

I have a red lamp.

_____

_____

_____

I have a blue lamp. _____

I have a green lamp. _____

I have a big lamp. _____

I have a cute lamp. _____

# CRAB

NAME: _____

crab crab crab crab
crab crab
crab crab
crab crab crab crab

Write "crab" on the lines:

## crab_____

_____

Circle the "crabs"

clap    camp    clap    crab

clap    clam    crab    crab

# I LIKE CRABS

NAME: _____

I like crabs.
I like crabs.
I like crabs.

_____

_____

_____

Crabs are red. _____
Crabs are blue. _____
Crabs are tasty. _____
Crabs live in the sea.

_____

# CLAM

clam clam clam
clam clam clam
clam clam clam clam
clam clam clam clam

Write "clam" on the lines:

## clam _____

_____

Circle the "clams"

clap     camp     clap     crab

clap     clam     crab     clam

# I LIKE CLAMS

NAME: _____

I like clams.
I like clams.
I like clams.

_____

_____

_____

Clams are cool. _____
Clams are big. _____
Clams are small. _____
Clams and crabs live in the sea.

_____

# MILK

milk milk milk milk
milk milk milk milk
milk milk milk milk

Write "milk" on the lines:

**milk**_____

_____

Circle the "milks"

milk    math    maze    milk

moth    mail    milk    men

# I DRINK MILK

NAME: _____

I drink milk.
I drink milk.
I drink milk.

_____

_____

_____

I drink tea. _____
I drink water. _____
I drink cola. _____
I drink juice. _____

# PINK

NAME: _____

pink pink pink pink pink
pink pink pink
pink pink pink
pink pink pink

Write "pink" on the lines:

pink_____

_____

Circle the "pinks"

pink   sink   play   pink

pans   ink   pink   pins

# I LIKE PINK

NAME: _____

I like pink.
I like pink.
I like pink.

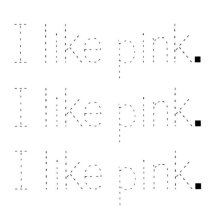

_____

_____

_____

I like blue too.

_____

I like red, orange, and green.

_____

I like black, yellow, and purple.

_____

# ART

NAME: _____

art art art art
art art art art
art art art art
art art art art art art

Write "art" on the lines:

art_____

_____

Circle the "arts"

art     arm     car     art

cart     farm     art     art

# I LIKE ART CLASS

## NAME: _____

I like Art class.
I like Art class.
I like Art class.

_____

_____

_____

I use a pencil. _____
I use markers. _____
I use crayons. _____
I use a paintbrush. _____

# ARM

arm arm arm arm arm
arm arm arm
arm arm arm
arm arm arm

Write "arm" on the lines:

**arm**_____

_____

Circle the "arms"

arm      arm    car    arm

cart    farm    ant    arm

# MY ARM IS BIG

NAME: _____

My arm is big.
My arm is big.
My arm is big.

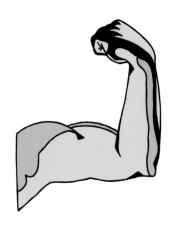

_____

_____

_____

My hand is big. _____
My foot is big. _____
My head is big. _____
My body is big. _____

# CAR

NAME: _____

car car

car car

car car car car car

car car car car car

Write "car" on the lines:

## car_____

_____

Circle the "cars"

car     arm     car     carp

cart     can     cart     car

# THE CAR IS FAST

NAME: _____

The car is fast.
The car is fast.
The car is fast.

_____

_____

_____

Cars are big. _____
Cars are red. _____
Cars are green. _____
Cars are white. _____

# CART

cart cart cart
cart cart cart
cart cart cart
cart cart cart cart

Write "cart" on the lines:

**cart**_____

_____

Circle the "carts"

clap    card    cart    carp

clap    cart    crab    cart

# I USE A CART

NAME: _____

I use a cart.
I use a cart.
I use a cart.

_____

_____

_____

I get an apple. _____
I get a banana. _____
I get some milk. _____
I get some fish. _____

# CARP

NAME: _____

carp carp carp
carp carp carp
carp carp carp
carp carp carp

Write "carp" on the lines:

## carp_____

_____

Circle the "carps"

carp   cart   caps   carp

carp   clam   cart   carp

# I LIKE THE CARP

NAME: _____

I like the carp.
I like the carp.
I like the carp.

_____

_____

_____

Carp are big. _____
Carp are white. _____
Carp are orange. _____
Carp are cool. _____

# PARK

NAME: _____

park park park park
park park
park park
park park

Write "park" on the lines:

**park**_____

_____

Circle the "parks"

panda    carp    camp    park

pork    pans    park    park

# I GO TO THE PARK

NAME: _____

I go to the park.
I go to the park.
I go to the park.

_____

_____

_____

I like to run. _____
I like to jump. _____
I like to swim. _____
I like to play. _____

Made in the USA
San Bernardino, CA
25 October 2017